With grateful thanks to my Israeli friends, whose unfailing hospitality and kindness helped me to understand and love the new Israel.

And thanks, also, to Sylvia Landress, Director of Zionist Archives and Library of the Palestine Foundation Fund in New York, and to David I. Marmor, Head of Research Department, Israel Office of Information, for their help and advice, and for the use of their picture files.

FIRST PRINTING

Printed in the United States of America by the Polygraphic Company of America

Published in Canada by Ambassador Books, Ltd., Toronto 1, Ontario

Library of Congress Catalog Card Number : 53-8609

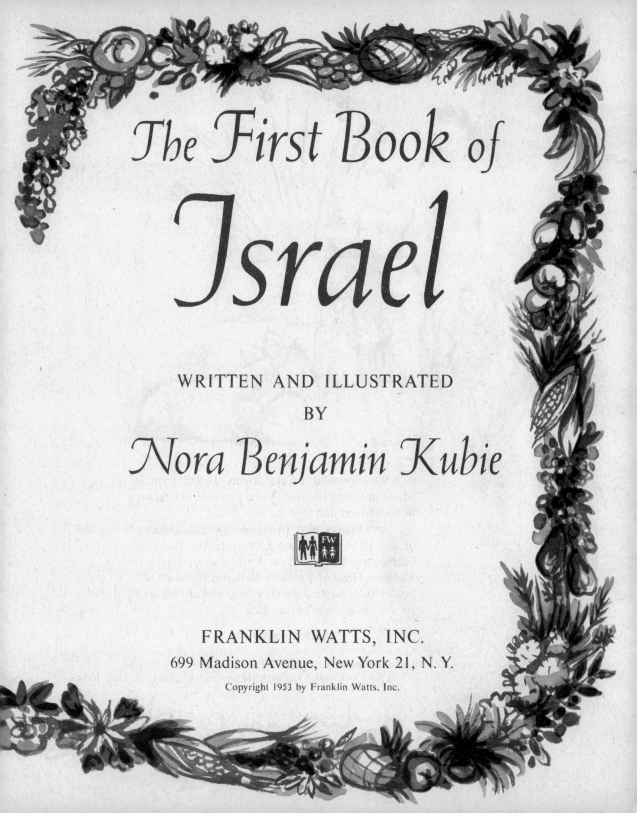

The First Book of
Israel

WRITTEN AND ILLUSTRATED

BY

Nora Benjamin Kubie

FRANKLIN WATTS, INC.

699 Madison Avenue, New York 21, N. Y.

Moses and the Land of Canaan

Long ago, there stood on the slopes of Mount Nebo, at the western edge of the Arabian desert, a man with white hair, flowing beard, and wise, far-seeing eyes. His name was Moses. From the mountain top he could see across the River Jordan into the land which the Lord had promised to his people. Moses had brought the Children of Israel out of slavery in Egypt. He had given them God's laws by which they were to live, and had led them for forty years through the wilderness. Now at last the land of

6

Canaan, flowing with milk and honey, was in sight, but Moses could not enter it. He was one hundred and twenty years old, the Bible tells us. He was tired and ready to die. He had appointed another leader to bring the Israelite tribes into their Promised Land.

Where Canaan once was, is now the modern state of Israel. Israel is the land of King David and King Solomon and the Hebrew prophets; the land where Jesus was born and died; a holy land for Jews and Christians. You can read the history of its beginnings in the Bible, and its present history in the daily papers. Between then and now, more than three thousand years have passed.

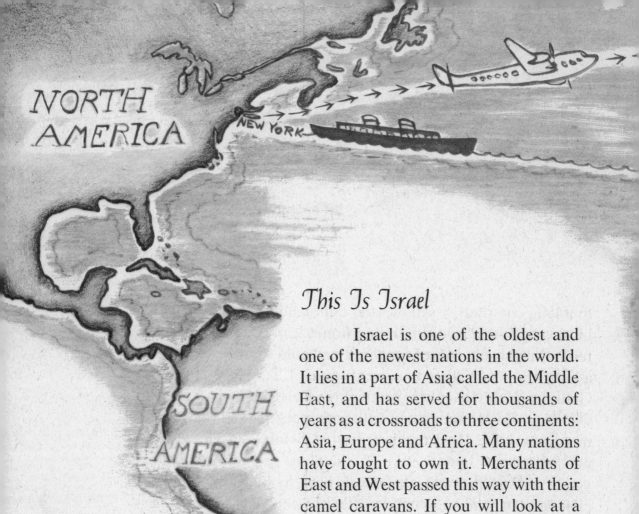

This Is Israel

Israel is one of the oldest and one of the newest nations in the world. It lies in a part of Asia called the Middle East, and has served for thousands of years as a crossroads to three continents: Asia, Europe and Africa. Many nations have fought to own it. Merchants of East and West passed this way with their camel caravans. If you will look at a map, you will see how small it is, not even as large as the state of Vermont.

If you were to go there by water, you would be on board the ship for at least two weeks. But you can reach Israel from New York in thirty-two flying hours—a day, a night, and part of another day. Perhaps you would fly via the Israel Airline, El Al. "El Al" means "skyward." If your plane should fly skyward to 20,000 feet, you would be able to see almost all of this little country from the air.

You would come in over the brilliant blue Mediterranean

8

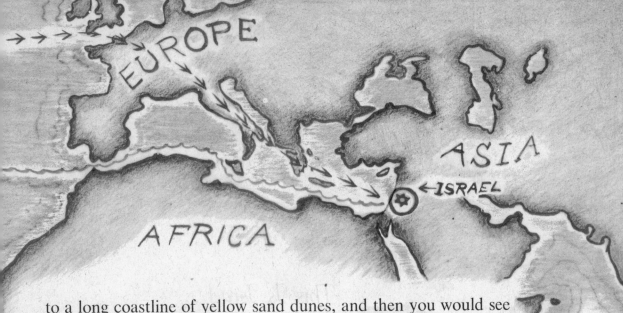

to a long coastline of yellow sand dunes, and then you would see
hills, valleys, and fields like a jigsaw puzzle of emerald green, mus-
tard yellow, gold, and red-brown. You would see the River Jordan,
a blue string with three blue beads on it: Lake Huleh, the Sea of
Galilee, and the Dead Sea. South of the Dead Sea is the Negev, the
wilderness — red and yellow and gray, pockmarked, barren as a
moon landscape. Here and there is a lonely tuft of green, one of the
new settlements in the desert. As the plane began to come down,
you would see cities and villages: old ones, looking as if they'd been
piled in a heap, and new ones, neatly laid out like a game of check-
ers. There would be a railroad connecting some of them, and a net-
work of roads.

Probably the sun would be shining on every roof-top, street
and field. It seldom rains here in summer. In October, the rains
begin, and torrents of water rush through every gully. It is never
really cold except in mountain towns, and between showers the sun
peeps out. In April, "the winter is past, the rain is over and gone;
the flowers appear on the earth; the time of the singing of birds is
come." It is summer again in Israel.

9

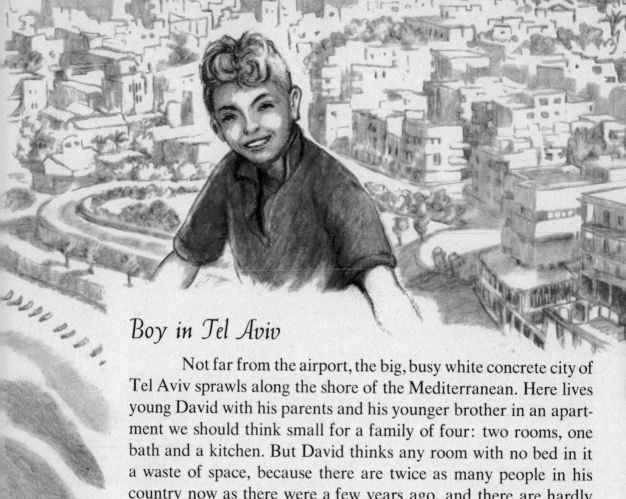

Boy in Tel Aviv

Not far from the airport, the big, busy white concrete city of Tel Aviv sprawls along the shore of the Mediterranean. Here lives young David with his parents and his younger brother in an apartment we should think small for a family of four: two rooms, one bath and a kitchen. But David thinks any room with no bed in it a waste of space, because there are twice as many people in his country now as there were a few years ago, and there are hardly enough rooms to go round. After all, David has the balcony on which to play. From there he can lean out and talk to his friends in the street without having to run down four flights of stairs. There are almost no elevators in Tel Aviv. The city was planned to spread out, instead of up, and so there are no tall buildings to cast shadows across the sunny streets.

David has blond curly hair and freckles all over his snub nose because he is out in the sun so much. He speaks Hebrew, and

10

also English, which is the language of his parents, who come from the English-speaking Union of South Africa. He is studying English in school too, as well as arithmetic, science, history and geography. And even though he is a city child, he is learning how to make things grow in the school garden. Part of the schoolyard is paved, so that David and the other boys and girls can play ball. David loves school. He goes to a public school, and by law he must go till he is thirteen. Then he hopes to go on to high school and the University.

Today is a special day, and there is no school. It is Independence Day. Everybody is out on the street celebrating. Each child waves his blue and white flag proudly. David is so happy he could dance, and pretty soon he is doing it, joining in a circle that goes round and round, jumping and stamping. It is the Hora, the folk dance of Israel. Faster and faster whirls the circle, boys and girls with their arms on each other's shoulders. They have no breath left to sing, but the bystanders sing for the dancers, clapping their hands in time. Then they sing a more serious song, known in many lands before the modern state of Israel came into existence. It is now the national anthem.

HATIKVAH

הַתִּקְוָה

KOL OD BA·LE·VAV P'NI··· MAH NE·FESH TE·HU DI HO MI·YAH U

LFA TE MIZ RACH KA DI·MAN A·YIN LE·ZI·ON ZO·PHI·YAH

OD LO AV DAH TIK·VA TE NU TIK·VAT SH'NAT·AL·PA··· YIM U·K'AM

CHAF·SHI BE·AR·ZE·NU BE·E·REZ ZI·ON VI YRU·SHA·LA··YIM.

O while within a Jewish
breast
Beats true a Jewish
heart,
And Jewish glances
turning East
To Zion fondly dart—
O then our Hope it is
not dead
Hope of two thousand
years,
To be free men in our
homestead
In Zion and Jerusalem.

כָּל·עוֹד בַּלֵּבָב פְּנִימָה

נֶפֶשׁ יְהוּדִי הוֹמִיָּה,

וּלְפַאֲתֵי מִזְרָח קָדִימָה

עַיִן לְצִיּוֹן צוֹפִיָּה–

עוֹד לֹא אָבְדָה תִקְוָתֵנוּ

הַתִּקְוָה שְׁנוֹת אַלְפַּיִם:

לִהְיוֹת עַם חָפְשִׁי בְּאַרְצֵנוּ,

בְּאֶרֶץ צִיּוֹן וִירוּשָׁלָיִם.

DAVID AND THE FLAG OF ISRAEL

David is named for David the King, who lived almost three thousand years ago. He was a shepherd lad who wrote the songs known as Psalms, killed the giant Goliath with a slingshot, and became ruler of all Israel. The insignia painted on his shield was a six-pointed star.

The flag of modern Israel is a blue Star of David and two blue stripes on a white ground.

Mount Zion is a hill at Jerusalem upon which King David built his fortress. The name "Zion" in time came to mean Jerusalem, or all the land of Israel.

Israel's branch of the International Red Cross, the organization which cares for people who are hurt in battle, floods, fires or other disasters, is the Red Star of David.

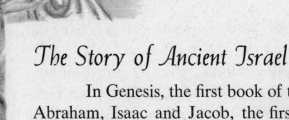

The Story of Ancient Israel

In Genesis, the first book of the Bible, you can read about Abraham, Isaac and Jacob, the first ancestors of the Israelites. Jacob wrestled one night with a messenger of the Lord, and when morning came, he was told that his name was no longer to be Jacob, but Israel, "he that striveth with God"—one who demands justice from both God and man. Jacob's descendants were called "the Children of Israel."

After the Children of Israel came with Moses from Egypt, they governed themselves through their chosen leaders. From this time, and from the teachings of later leaders, the Prophets, come the ideas on which the new state is founded: peace, justice, democracy, and freedom from want for all.

The Israelite tribes united into one kingdom, but after the death of King Solomon, about 1000 B.C., the country split into two: the Northern Kingdom of Israel, and the Southern Kingdom of Judah. Both were strong, prosperous states, whose riches were envied by their neighbors. Two hundred years later, the Northern Kingdom was conquered by its warlike neighbors, the Assyrians. No one knows what happened to its people. They are known as the "Lost Tribes of Israel."

A hundred and fifty years after that, Nebuchadnezzar, King of Babylon, invaded Judah and fought for ten long years. At last Nebuchadnezzar took Jerusalem, the capital city, destroyed the Temple which Solomon had built, carried away its treasures,

14

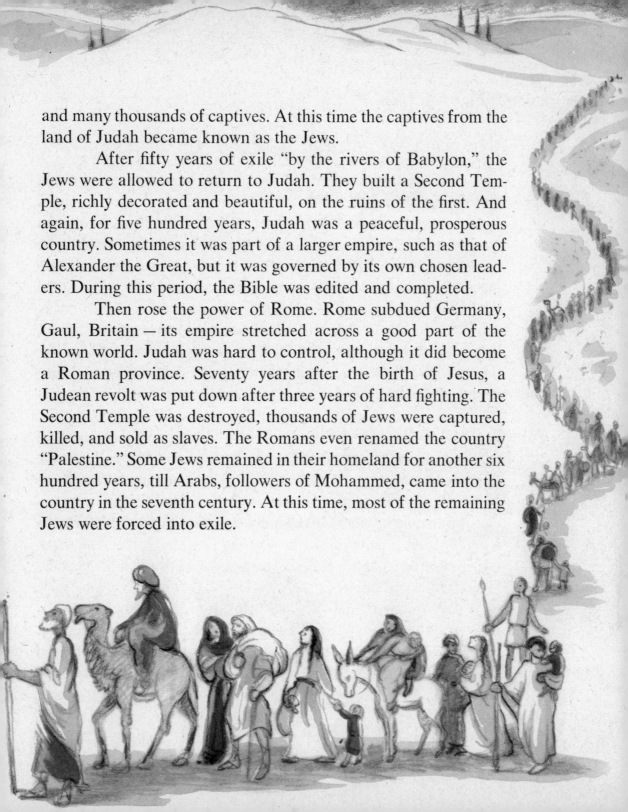

and many thousands of captives. At this time the captives from the land of Judah became known as the Jews.

After fifty years of exile "by the rivers of Babylon," the Jews were allowed to return to Judah. They built a Second Temple, richly decorated and beautiful, on the ruins of the first. And again, for five hundred years, Judah was a peaceful, prosperous country. Sometimes it was part of a larger empire, such as that of Alexander the Great, but it was governed by its own chosen leaders. During this period, the Bible was edited and completed.

Then rose the power of Rome. Rome subdued Germany, Gaul, Britain — its empire stretched across a good part of the known world. Judah was hard to control, although it did become a Roman province. Seventy years after the birth of Jesus, a Judean revolt was put down after three years of hard fighting. The Second Temple was destroyed, thousands of Jews were captured, killed, and sold as slaves. The Romans even renamed the country "Palestine." Some Jews remained in their homeland for another six hundred years, till Arabs, followers of Mohammed, came into the country in the seventh century. At this time, most of the remaining Jews were forced into exile.

How the New State Came to Be

Though the followers of Mohammed ruled Palestine, the Jews still called it "Eretz Israel"—the land of Israel. From time to time throughout the centuries Jews came back as pilgrims, and also returned to settle.

The rest of the Jews were scattered all over the world. Keeping their Jewish religion, they became loyal citizens of many countries. In the United States, Jews are Americans, just as Catholics, Quakers and Mormons are Americans.

In some countries they were badly treated. They were forced to live in a special part of town called a ghetto, surrounded by a wall. They were not allowed to work with their hands, and they could not work on the land. Often they were tortured to make them give up their religion.

Why did this happen to Jews? Some say it was because they were different from the people around them. They refused to become Christians or Moslems, and they insisted, in their pri-

16

vate lives, on keeping certain rules, in living according to the old law of the Bible. Differences of costume and special badges were forced on them. Mysterious stories, quite untrue, grew up about their form of worship.

It was easy to be cruel to Jews, scattered as they were, and therefore a weak, unarmed group in each country. In Russia, toward the end of the last century, many innocent men, women and children were killed in the ghettos. Those who could, fled. Some came to America. Others believed that they could be safe only in "Eretz Israel."

Many Russian Jews escaped to Palestine. They bought barren, stony land from the Arab landowners, who were glad to sell to them. Palestine's soil had been stripped bare, and it was no longer a land of milk and honey. But the Jewish settlers began to restore it. They built settlements and made farms in the wilderness, like the pioneers of early American days. They too called themselves pioneers—"Hallutzim."

Hope began to grow that Palestine, then a part of the Turkish Empire,

might one day again be a Jewish state. Those who believed in this idea and worked for it were called "Zionists."

Turkey fought on the side of Germany in World War I, and was defeated. A regiment of Palestinian Jews fought as part of the British Army against the Turks. In 1917, Lord Balfour, the British Secretary of Foreign Affairs, issued a declaration of sympathy with Zionist hopes. England, he said, "views with favor the establishment in Palestine of a national home for the Jewish people." After the war, the League of Nations appointed Britain to govern Palestine until its people would again set up their own government.

And now, filled with hope, more Jews arrived in Palestine. They planted trees, irrigated dry fields, drained marshes. Prosperous farms and settlements sprang up in many parts of the country.

Meanwhile a new war was on the way in Europe. Hitler was the ruler of Germany, and Mussolini of Italy. Neither believed in democracy and freedom. Because the Jews stood up for the rights of man, Hitler hated them. He also found it convenient to blame on them everything that went wrong in Germany. His two announced purposes were to conquer the world and to kill all the Jews.

Some Jews escaped to countries where they were safe, like England and America. But these countries no longer welcomed an unlimited number of people from foreign lands. For some Jews, Palestine was the only place to which they could go. Others preferred to go there.

In Germany, and wherever Hitler's armies marched, Jews were thrown in prison camps and murdered. Six million of them died by the end of World War II. Palestine Jews again fought in the British Army and, toward the end of the war, had their own Jewish brigade. Afterwards they came home to Palestine and again worked hard to improve the land. There were many more of them now, and even more wanted to come.

The Arabs did not want them to come. The rich Arab land-owners did not like the Western ideas which the Jews brought with them: better wages for workers, equal rights for women, better education for all. Arabs attacked Jewish settlements, and the Jews fought back.

The British yielded to Arab demands to limit sharply the number of Jews who might now come into Palestine. They claimed to be trying to prevent bloodshed between Arabs and Jews, but they went back on Lord Balfour's declaration, which the League of Nations had expected them to put into practice. But in spite of well-trained British soldiers, a half-secret fighting force of Jews, the Haganah, brought in the immigrants. Finally Britain took the quarrel to the United Nations, which decided that Palestine was to be divided. One part was to become an independent Arab state, and the other, an independent Jewish state. The British officials left the country. And so, on the evening of May 14, 1948, the new state of Israel was born.

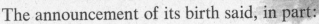

ITED NATIONS

ISRAEL

LEBANON
SYRIA
MEDITERRANEAN SEA
Lake Huleh
SAFED
HAIFA
GALILEE
SEA OF GALILEE
NAZARETH
JORDAN RIVER
TEL AVIV
JERUSALEM
MT. NEBO
DEAD SEA
BEERSHEBA
JORDAN
THE NEGEV
EGYPT
ELATH
RED SEA

The announcement of its birth said, in part:

The State of Israel will be open to the immigration of Jews from all the countries of their dispersion;

will promote the development of the country for the benefit of all its inhabitants;

will be based on the principles of liberty, justice and peace as conceived by the Prophets of Israel;

will uphold the full and political equality of all its citizens without distinction of religion, race or sex;

will safeguard the Holy Places of all religions;

and will loyally uphold the principles of the United Nations charter.

21

LEADERS OF ZIONISM
AND OF THE NEW ISRAEL

THEODOR HERZL, a Jew from Austria, devoted his life to promoting a new Jewish state, wrote books about it, asked kings and statesmen to support it. He called the first international meeting of Zionists in 1897. His dream came true long after his death, and he is buried in a national shrine near Jerusalem.

ELIAZER BEN YEHUDA, a frail, sickly young writer, went to Palestine in 1881. Owing to his efforts, Hebrew became a living language instead of a language found only in books. Ben Yehuda wrote the first modern Hebrew dictionary.

CHAIM WEIZMANN was elected first president of Israel in recognition of all he had done to advance the cause of Zionism, particularly in discussions with the British Government. He was respected all over the world for his work as a scientist. He died in 1952.

DAVID BEN-GURION, first prime minister of the state of Israel, went to Palestine in his youth as a pioneer. He helped to organize the Jewish Legion in World War I and was exiled by the Turks, but returned after the war. He devoted himself to building up the country for many years and is a great leader.

FIGHTERS FOR FREEDOM

MAJOR-GENERAL ORDE WINGATE, English officer, student of the Bible, fighter for freedom in many lands. Although not a Jew, he knew Hebrew well and called himself a Zionist. During the Arab riots in the 1930's, he taught the Jews commando tactics.

COLONEL DAVID MARCUS, born of poor orthodox Jewish parents on New York's East Side, won an appointment to the United States Military Academy at West Point. He served in the Pacific during World War II, and on General Marshall's staff. He went to Israel to help train the fighting Haganah. An Arab sniper's bullet killed him there. His men called him "Mickey"; the people of Israel knew him as "the American."

HANNAH SENESCH, born in Hungary, went to Palestine in 1939 and worked in a farm settlement. She volunteered for secret missions with the British Army in World War II, was parachuted into enemy country, taken prisoner, and shot. She was only twenty-three years old. This is a poem she wrote:

"Blessed is the match that is consumed in kindling flame.
Blessed is the flame that burns in the secret fastness of the heart.
Blessed is the heart with strength to stop its beating for honor's sake.
Blessed is the match that is consumed in kindling flame."

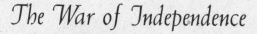

The War of Independence

David remembers the first Day of Independence well, even though he was a very little boy then. Everybody was dancing in the streets that night, parents and their children together. And he remembers the following day, too, when bombing planes from Egypt came over the house. For the Arab nations which surround Israel refused to obey the United Nations' decision that part of Palestine was to be a Jewish state. Seven of them, helped by Arabs within Israel's new boundaries, and plentifully supplied with tanks, planes and heavy guns, attacked the infant state. At once the Haganah became the army of Israel. David remembers how his family sat listening to the radio as the voice of one of their leaders solemnly proclaimed the state of Israel. And how his mother helped his father to put on the army officer's uniform which had been made ready weeks before. The next day he went off to war, and the family never knew when or if they would see him again.

24

David is not likely to forget any of this, but besides there is a reminder—the brick wall, hastily put up, which still stands before the entrance to his apartment house. Often when he started off for nursery school in the morning with his mother they would have to dodge behind the wall to escape the fire of Arab machine guns shooting from the mosque tower in neighboring Jaffa down into the streets of Tel Aviv.

You see, the Israel War of Independence wasn't in 1776, but just a few years ago. May 14, 1948 fell on the fifth day of the month of Iyar, according to the Jewish calendar. This is celebrated by all Israelis, as citizens of Israel are called, as Independence Day.

New City and Ancient Harbor

Last summer an American child named Susan went with her parents to visit Israel. David's father, who had returned from the army, knew Susan's father through business. So the two families got together.

"Hello," said Susan to David.

"Shalom," said David to Susan.

"Shalom" means "peace." In Israel, people use this word for hello and good-by. Peace means a great deal to them.

David took Susan sightseeing in Tel Aviv. Allenby Street was noisy and crowded with shoppers carrying string market bags. It didn't look too different from the California town in which Susan lived. There were drug stores and clothing stores and souvenir shops, a great many bookstores, but no super markets. There were houses of worship such as a big new synagogue and a little musty old one.

Down a side street went David, and out on another boulevard, with Susan panting to keep up. Each minute he was pointing out something that was new and wonderful. He showed her a movie house, featuring an American Western, and the famous Habima Theater, offering a Shakespearean play in Hebrew the next night and a concert by the Israel Symphony Orchestra on the following one. He was about to show her the Art Museum when Susan went on strike.

"Phew!" she said, "I'm *hot*—and thirsty. Couldn't we have a soda?"

"But of course." David led her

27

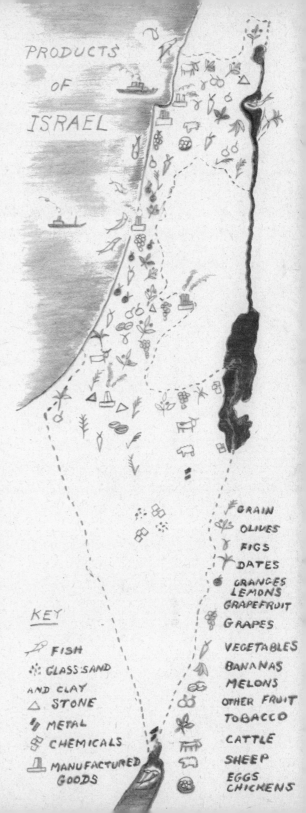

PRODUCTS

OF

ISRAEL

KEY

FISH

GLASS·SAND
AND CLAY

STONE

METAL

CHEMICALS

MANUFACTURED
GOODS

GRAIN

OLIVES

FIGS

DATES

ORANGES
LEMONS
GRAPEFRUIT

GRAPES

VEGETABLES

BANANAS

MELONS

OTHER FRUIT

TOBACCO

CATTLE

SHEEP

EGGS
CHICKENS

into an outdoor café where people were drinking tea from glasses while they read their newspapers. David and Susan sat down, and he gave an order. The waiter brought him a glass of orange juice and Susan one of pink bubbling water.

"What's this?" Susan asked.

"'Gazoz'—soda, which you asked for," David said. Politely he pointed to his own glass. "Would you rather have 'mitz'? Or an ice?"

Susan thought she'd try the gazoz. It tasted slightly of raspberry juice, was sweet and cold. "Not bad," she said.

David pulled her to her feet. "Come, Shoshanna, we take the bus to Jaffa. That will be different for you."

"Shoshanna?" Susan looked puzzled.

"It's Hebrew for Susanna. Do you mind?" David asked.

Susan thought Shoshanna was a pretty name.

"Shosh for short," David said.

"That's not so pretty," Susan answered.

People were standing in line for the bus. Susan giggled. "Look at that old gentleman," she whispered, "in shorts, just like yours—and no tie—in the *city!*"

"Why not?" said David. "Don't you think it's sensible for one to dress comfortably in summer, even for business? My father wears shorts to the office too."

Susan had to admit that it was sensible.

The bus took them by bumpy stages to Jaffa.

Jaffa used to be an Arab town. When Israel began to win the war, most of the Arabs grew frightened and ran away. Jewish people who had no homes moved into the little houses of pink, blue and yellow plaster which, piled up like children's blocks, looked almost ready to tumble down into the bright blue sea. There was no electricity in those houses, David said. No telephones or running water or bathrooms.

"Goodness!" said Susan. "How dreadful!"

"We can't make everything new at once," David said. "Besides, some of the old things are interesting." For instance, he told her, Jaffa was Joppa in Bible times, the very port from which Jonah had sailed on the unfortunate voyage during which he met the whale. This afternoon there was a steamship in the harbor loading oranges.

The street went up hill and down dale, narrow and winding, smelling of charcoal fires, fish and no plumbing. Susan stopped to pet a small donkey which pulled a load of furniture big enough to furnish one of the houses. A motorcycle-driven cart almost ran her down. Then she had to squeeze herself quickly against a wall as a big truck roared through.

From low, dark doorways, children stared curiously at the American child, and Susan stared back. They spoke to David, but she couldn't understand what they said. There were carroty-haired children, and children with hair like skeins of tangled yellow silk.

There were children as dark as Negroes, and bare-footed, ragged, coffee-colored children with huge black eyes and earrings in their small pierced ears.

"Are they Arabs?" Susan asked.

"No, they are Jews from oriental countries," David said. "There *are* still some Arabs here, but we do not any longer have to be afraid that they will shoot us. See, there is one, in the balloon trousers and the red fez on his head, smoking his water-pipe in front of his shop so peacefully."

A terrible squawking sounded from the end of the street. "The bus, the bus!" David cried, seizing Susan's hand, and breaking into a run. "No buses run here on Friday evenings or all day Saturday, so we'd better catch this one if we don't want to walk back to Tel Aviv!"

31

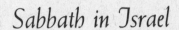

Sabbath in Israel

Susan and her parents had been invited to have Friday night supper with David's family. The table was laid with a fresh white linen cloth, a bowl of flowers, silver candlesticks, a new-baked loaf of bread, and a bottle of wine. In the ancient nation, wine was much used. It was cleaner and safer to drink than water. Grape growing and wine making are still important industries.

David had changed his jersey for a clean white shirt. His blond curls were slicked down, and his face was scrubbed so that every freckle showed. His little brother Reuben and his father and mother too were dressed up. David's mother looked excited and happy when she came from the kitchen and motioned everyone to sit down at the table.

David's mother lit the candles and said a blessing. Even though she couldn't understand the Hebrew words, Susan felt at home. She was accustomed to grace before meals.

" 'Shabbat Shalom,' " said David to Susan.

"That means, 'May you have a peaceful Sabbath,' " his father said. "It is always our greeting on the Sabbath Eve." He went on to explain that the day of rest in Israel was from sundown on Friday till sundown Saturday. "If you are a believing Jew, you go to services in the synagogue. But in any case, you spend much time at home with your family. The commandment says one may work six days out of the week, but on the seventh one must rest—the master, the servant, and even the animals." He smiled. "Like many of the old laws, it is a sensible rule."

"We rest on Sunday," Susan's mother said.

"Yes, you Gentiles changed the day of rest to the first day of the week, but here we go according to the Torah, the ancient law of the Bible, in many things."

Even meat had to be butchered in a certain way called "kosher," he continued. Cooking and serving meat was also kosher in army camps and institutions. In private homes, however, food was cooked and served entirely according to the family's own choice and belief.

"I hope you will like our choice," David's mother said.

First there was stuffed fish. Then there were some small pieces of chicken, and a big salad of eggplant, juicy red tomatoes,

and crisp sliced cucumbers. For dessert there were tiny stewed apricots, called "mish-mish."

"My goodness," Susan said, "it doesn't seem as if food was scarce, as David said."

His mother smiled gently. "I'm afraid we don't eat so well as this always, for we have not yet raised enough food in our new country for all the people. But we save up all week so as to have a good dinner on Shabbat."

Then she went to the piano and sang a Sabbath Eve song written in the town of Safad in Palestine, four hundred years ago:

"Come, my friend, to meet the bride,
For it is a well-spring of blessing.
Let us welcome the presence of the Sabbath…"

THE LANGUAGE OF ISRAEL

The people who came to Israel began by speaking different languages. There had to be a national language that all could learn, so that they could understand each other. So Hebrew, the language in which the Old Testament was originally written, was revived. New words had to be made up for such things as airplanes and refrigerators, which didn't exist at the time of the Bible. The Israelis had to go to school to learn their own language. Now almost all of them, even the old folks, speak some Hebrew. A child born in Israel, of course, speaks Hebrew just as naturally as you speak English.

Although the Hebrew Alphabet is called the Alef-Bet, the letters are not like ours. Hebrew is written and read from right to left, instead of from left to right as in English and other European languages.

Bet (בּ) is like B, and it also means "house."

The word for refrigerator is "M'karir."

The word for airplane is "Aviron."

"Ha" is the word for "the." The boy child is "hayelled." The girl child is "hayalda."

Lesson is "she-oor."

Teacher is "moreh."

It is not hard to learn Hebrew if you have a good teacher.

SOME HOLIDAYS

In late January or early February, TU B'SHVAT, the New Year of the Trees, or Arbor Day. Children go out into the woods, singing, to plant trees.

In March, PURIM. Long ago the king of Persia married a beautiful Jewess, Esther. Queen Esther prevented wicked Haman's plot to kill the Jews of Persia. On Purim, in the synagogue, children use a rattle to drown out Haman's name whenever it is mentioned. Fancy dress parties are held on Purim and presents are given to friends and to the poor.

A Purim Rattle

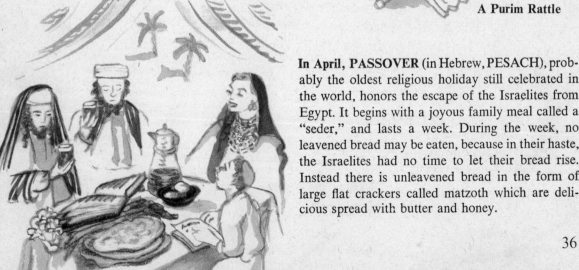

In April, PASSOVER (in Hebrew, PESACH), probably the oldest religious holiday still celebrated in the world, honors the escape of the Israelites from Egypt. It begins with a joyous family meal called a "seder," and lasts a week. During the week, no leavened bread may be eaten, because in their haste, the Israelites had no time to let their bread rise. Instead there is unleavened bread in the form of large flat crackers called matzoth which are delicious spread with butter and honey.

36

IN ISRAEL

HAD GADYO — A Song for Children on Seder Eve

An only kid, an only kid,
That father bought for two small
coins,
An only kid, an only kid.

Then came the cat and ate the
kid . . .

Then came the dog and bit the cat
That ate the kid . . .

Then came the stick and beat
the dog
That bit the cat that ate the kid . . .

Then came the fire and burned
the stick
That beat the dog that bit the cat
That ate the kid . . .

Then came the water and put out
the fire
That burned the stick that beat
the dog
That bit the cat that ate the kid . . .

Then came the ox and drank
the water
That put out the fire that burned
the stick
That beat the dog that bit the cat
That ate the kid . . .

Then came the butcher and
slaughtered the ox
That drank the water that put out
the fire
That beat the dog that bit the cat
That ate the kid . . .

Then came the Angel of Death and
killed the butcher
That slaughtered the ox that drank
the water
That put out the fire that burned
the stick
That beat the dog that bit the cat
That ate the kid . . .

Then came the blessed Holy One
and killed the Angel of Death
That killed the butcher that
slaughtered the ox
That drank the water that put out
the fire
That burned the stick that beat
the dog
That bit the cat that ate the kid
That father bought for two small
coins
An only kid, an only kid.

EGG AND
SALT WATER

BITTER
HERBS

HAGGADAH

HAROSETH

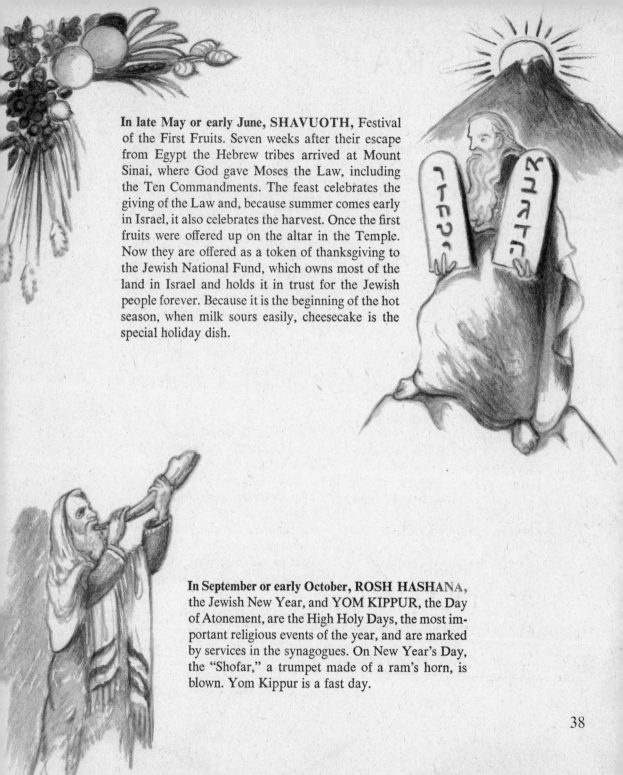

In late May or early June, SHAVUOTH, Festival of the First Fruits. Seven weeks after their escape from Egypt the Hebrew tribes arrived at Mount Sinai, where God gave Moses the Law, including the Ten Commandments. The feast celebrates the giving of the Law and, because summer comes early in Israel, it also celebrates the harvest. Once the first fruits were offered up on the altar in the Temple. Now they are offered as a token of thanksgiving to the Jewish National Fund, which owns most of the land in Israel and holds it in trust for the Jewish people forever. Because it is the beginning of the hot season, when milk sours easily, cheesecake is the special holiday dish.

In September or early October, ROSH HASHANA, the Jewish New Year, and YOM KIPPUR, the Day of Atonement, are the High Holy Days, the most important religious events of the year, and are marked by services in the synagogues. On New Year's Day, the "Shofar," a trumpet made of a ram's horn, is blown. Yom Kippur is a fast day.

38

In October, SUCCOTH, the Feast of Tabernacles, a week of thanksgiving for the autumn harvest. There is feasting in booths decorated with autumn leaves and fruits, because during their journey from Egypt, the tribes dwelt in tabernacles, or booths. In the old days, since this holiday came at a time when the autumn rains were expected, it was also a Feast of Water-drawing.

In mid-winter, HANUKAH, the Feast of Lights. Judas Maccabaeus and his family led a successful revolt against King Antiochus of Syria in the second century B. C. When the Temple was cleansed after the Maccabees' victory, one day's supply of holy oil miraculously burned for eight days. To celebrate this holiday in Jewish homes, a candle is lit, then one more each day for eight days, till eight candles are alight. In Israel relay runners of the national sports club light a torch at Mode'in, the town of the Maccabees, on the first day of Hanukah. They carry it all the way to Jerusalem, over mountain and valley, to kindle a big eight-branched candlestick.

Hanukah is a time for parties and present giving. The special present for children is a spinning top with four sides upon which are letters that stand for "a great miracle happened here."

Shoes and Ships—Haifa

David's father and Susan's father drove to Haifa to see a factory in which both were interested. David and Susan came along, and they all stopped first for a swim at a beach on the way. Steps led down between steep cliffs to the yellow sand and the blue-green sea. It seemed to Susan that there were hundreds of children shouting and splashing each other or building sand-castles while their mothers watched lazily. They were all sizes, ages and colors, but mostly toast-colored from the sun. Young men with bulging muscles sat in a circle tossing around a heavy ball, or struggled to lift up at arm's length a heavy weight to show how strong they were. The game seemed to be to see how long they could hold it without dropping it.

David opened the beach bag and took out a small rubber ball and two ping-pong bats. When he and Susan had changed into their swim suits, he taught her the game that was going on fast and furiously all over the beach. It was harder than ping-pong because the ball could not bounce on the sand and had to be kept flying from bat to bat.

Then they went for a swim in the warm clear water. Far out on the blue horizon were the white sails of two fishing boats. Closer inshore was a rocky islet, and those who had swum out and were clinging to it looked like mermaids with their tails still in the water. There were also surf boats, shaped like bananas sliced lengthways, which were guided through the waves with long double paddles. It looked exciting. After lunch the fathers said it was time to go to Haifa.

There are factories for all sorts of things in Haifa: shoes, cement, nails and screws, pots and pans, cotton goods. Susan saw an American-designed car and several other familiar things which were being made in Haifa. Most of the factories are new, for there were almost none in Palestine till the Jews came there in great numbers.

The first united federation of Jewish workers, called Histadrut, was formed in Haifa in 1920. Histadrut is a labor union like no other in the world. It owns many of the factories and shops, provides its members with doctors, dental clinics, insurance, and rest homes; publishes books and a newspaper; and has a workers' theater. It is both a union of working men and a company in which all its members hold shares.

Haifa is a beautiful city. Mount Carmel, thickly clustered with white houses, modern apartments and hotels, rises steeply from the edge of a vast, crescent-shaped blue bay. A breakwater protects the inner harbor. Ships from many lands jostle each other along the docks. Derricks whine, and porters tramp back and forth, loading cargoes of things that Israel sells abroad, unloading things it needs to import.

The Nautical School and the Technion, a big engineering college, are both in Haifa. David's uncle Gad, a graduate of the Nautical School, is now an officer in the Israel Navy.

Before Israel was a nation, Gad had captained one of the small battered ships that brought refugees secretly from Europe to Palestine. Often these poor people, even the sick and old ones, had to wade ashore at some deserted beach, perhaps the very one where Susan and David had been swimming so gaily. There members of the Haganah met them and took them in trucks to a safe hiding place. Some were caught by the British and sent back to Europe or to camps on the island of Cyprus, and the ships were taken away from their owners. But Gad's ship came through safely.

Now ships sail openly into Haifa Bay with people from all over the world. This is the "Ingathering of the Exiles." Many are poor, sick, too old or too young to work for a living. They are given shelter, food, medicine, and care. In its first four years, the number of people in Israel doubled. Israel now has more than a million and a half people, about as many as the city of Los Angeles, California.

The Newcomers

David's father took Susan and David to see Esther, a young friend of his who lived with her parents in a "ma'abara." A ma'abara is a village of temporary houses in which newcomers live till permanent homes can be built for them. So many people have poured into Israel that this takes some time.

Esther's family had brought with them from Rumania their most precious possessions: a bulky carved chest and an old-fashioned sewing machine. In their one-room aluminum hut, Esther's father was busily using the sewing machine. He had already set himself up in business as a tailor.

When the family had first arrived, there were only tents in the ma'abara. It was winter, rainy and cold. So the children of the newcomers were taken to live in barracks at an army camp. Soldiers were their nurses and teachers. And that is how David's father had come to know Esther. Someday soon, her family hope to move to a real house of their own.

"Imagine an army adopting children!" Susan said.

"The children are kings in Israel," David's father said. "To them we always give the best, even if we do without—because they are our future."

In the next hut lived a family from the mountains of Kurdistan in Persia. The father was a big, fierce-looking man with a thick, bristling black beard and a blue turban.

The rows and rows of square metal huts, all exactly alike, did not look very homelike. But one had flowers planted in rusty tin cans by the doorstep, and a vine struggled to climb the hot shiny wall of another. A sandy-haired boy was watering the vine with a teapot. He was from Lithuania, he told David's father.

All these new neighbors are learning to speak Hebrew, so that they can talk to each other.

THE CITIZENS OF ISRAEL

The citizens of Israel are from seventy-four different countries.
There are Jews from:

Germany

France

England

the United States

Spain

Holland

Arabia

Russia

Poland

North Africa

Iran

Ethiopia

Iraq

India

China

There are also Arabs, who settled the country while it was under
Moslem rule and have lived there ever since.

THE GOVERNMENT OF ISRAEL

Israel is a republic governed by a congress, a president, a prime minister, and a group of government ministers called a cabinet.

Every Israeli citizen of 18 or older may vote for the 120 members of the congress, called the Knesset. This name means "assembly," and is taken from the "Great Assembly" of the people of Israel in the time of the second Temple.

The members of the Knesset elect the president.

The president receives foreign diplomats and signs bills passed by the Knesset. After consulting with members of the Knesset, he appoints the prime minister.

The Prime Minister chooses the members of his cabinet. (He calls it "forming a government.") The Prime Minister must have the confidence of the Knesset to maintain his government.

The cabinet, as well as any member of the Knesset, may suggest laws to the Knesset. The Knesset discusses and votes on them. The Government (prime minister and cabinet) carries them out.

47

A Village of Children

Nehemiah is a boy from Yemen, a little kingdom in a far-off corner of Arabia. In Biblical times, it was the land of Sheba, from which came the famous queen to visit King Solomon. Yemenite Jews, who claim their ancestors made the fine metal work for the doors of Solomon's Temple, are still good at making things.

The Moslems of Yemen treated them badly. So, when they heard of the new Israel, they packed what they could carry in bundles and set off to find it. They trekked across miles of desert to Aden, where big transport planes supplied by a committee of American Jews were waiting to fly them to Israel. Nehemiah was taken with his neighbors because he was an orphan.

Nehemiah had been brought up on the story that someday the Jews would go home to Zion "on the wings of eagles," so he

48

was not too surprised or frightened. But when the party had landed in Israel, and started off in the bus that was to take them from the airport to the newcomers' camp, one man cried out, "Surely something is wrong with this carriage—it will not rise from the ground!" The Yemenites had traveled with donkeys and camels and airplanes, but they had never known about automobiles!

If you had seen Nehemiah on his arrival, you would have thought him six years old instead of ten, so scrawny and pitiful was he. He was sent to a Children's Village with other boys who had no parents. A kind housemother taught him how to sleep in a bed, use a knife and fork, and take a bath. Living in the poorest quarter of a poor Arab town, he had never known any of these things.

He has been in the Children's Village four years now, and though he is still small, like most Yemenites, he is strong, bursting with health and gaiety. His dark eyes sparkle as he talks and he makes quick, graceful gestures. He shares a room with his three best friends: Yusef from French North Africa; Juan from Argentina; and blond Willy from Germany. They are very proud of their room, furnished with chairs and chests they made themselves.

There is also a cobbler's shop in the Village, where a jolly red-bearded shoemaker teaches the boys to make the shoes that the Village needs, a weaver's shop, and a machine repair shop.

The boys do all the work of their home and farm. They gather at meetings to make many of their own rules. They have four hours of school work a day, and there is still time for games and fun.

Nehemiah likes working in the machine shop best. The teacher smiles when he hears Nehemiah absent-mindedly whistling an ancient Yemenite folk song, full of sadness and longing. Nehemiah does not feel sad. Remembering the magic carpet which brought him from Arabia, he hopes to be an airplane mechanic when he leaves the Village at sixteen. Even though he has no mother or father, he thinks he is a lucky boy.

The Farmers

Dana thinks she is the luckiest girl in the world. She is a "sabra," which means prickly pear, fruit of the cactus hedges that grow along the roadsides. Children born in Israel are called sabras because they are prickly on the outside—a little rude and ready to fight—but sweet and good within.

Dana lives on a "kibbutz," a collective farm. On a kibbutz everything—houses, fields, machinery, animals, fruits and vegetables—is owned jointly by the people who live there. The planning and running of the farm are done by elected committees. When Dana needs a new pair of overalls, she simply asks for it at the storeroom.

The farm is in the Valley of Jezreel, which is usually called just Ha-Emek, or the Valley. When the Jewish pioneers came to Palestine, the Valley was a swamp. Its biggest crop was mosquitoes, which carried malaria to the people who lived there. The young pioneers dug ditches to drain off the water, planted trees, built houses and barns and silos. Now it is good farm country.

Dana's farm is really a village of several hundred families. But no family has a house of its own in this village. Dana's parents have only one room, but it is a well-furnished room with books and a radio, an electric fan and a teakettle. Some of the older couples have little flats to themselves, a room and a half and a private shower. Dana does not live with her parents but in the part of the farm called the Children's Republic, in a house with other children of her age. Children begin to look out for themselves very early, for in each house the chairs and tables are just the right size. The wash basins and showers and the hooks for toothbrushes and washcloths are at just the right height, so that no one has to ask for help.

There is, of course, a school in the Children's Republic. Dana's teacher is young and cheerful and makes the lessons more fun than work. Dana has jobs to do as well. She must pick up her toys when she is through playing, for they are not hers but everyone's. She helps set tables for meals in the Children's House, she waters the lawn outside, and she plants radishes. Sometimes she has to chase away a pet gazelle that loves to eat the crimson

roses. In summer there is a daily visit to a pool to swim. Dana
and her friends dive and swim and have water fights.

Dana's parents work hard, but in the late afternoon, when
work is done, they fetch Dana and then she is with them until it
is time for her to go to bed. She stays with them all day Saturday,
too. At those times, her parents have nothing to do but play with
her. And that is the way Dana thinks a family's life should be.
Her friends who live with her in the Children's House are her
family too.

Her mother works in the laundry, or helps to tidy up the
dining hall where all the grownups eat at long tables together.
The white walls are bright with paintings done by a kibbutz member, and the wide windows look out across the orchards and
many-colored fields. Friday nights there are white cloths and
flowers on the tables, and Dana comes there to sit with her parents.
Sometimes there are movies in the dining hall after supper, or
concerts or parties.

53

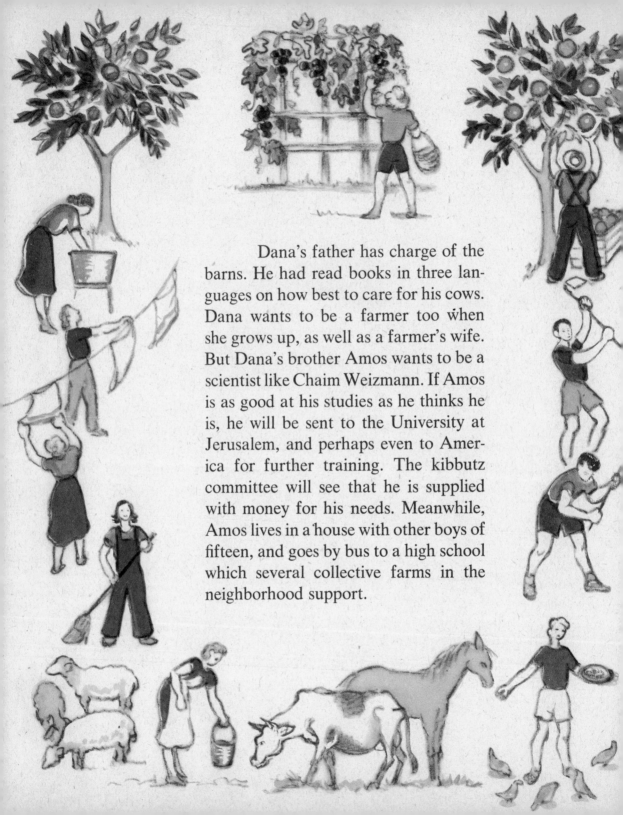

Dana's father has charge of the barns. He had read books in three languages on how best to care for his cows. Dana wants to be a farmer too when she grows up, as well as a farmer's wife. But Dana's brother Amos wants to be a scientist like Chaim Weizmann. If Amos is as good at his studies as he thinks he is, he will be sent to the University at Jerusalem, and perhaps even to America for further training. The kibbutz committee will see that he is supplied with money for his needs. Meanwhile, Amos lives in a house with other boys of fifteen, and goes by bus to a high school which several collective farms in the neighborhood support.

A few years ago, Amos went with a group of boys and a teacher on a hiking trip. All over Israel you will see hikers swinging along, usually singing, with their packs and their bedrolls on their backs. Amos and his group went to Degania, the first collective farm in Israel. One of the founders of Degania, more than forty years ago, was A. D. Gordon, a man who believed that Jews must return to the soil because only work with the hands, especially work on the land, made for a happy life. Gordon loved nature, and would often drop his hoe to pick a strange wildflower, or catch an insect that was new to him. His collection was the start of the Gordon Institute at Degania, a natural history museum which has preserved a specimen of every plant, bug, animal and snake in Israel. It was the Gordon Institute that gave Amos his desire to be a scientist.

Not all farms in Israel are collectives. There are also cooperative villages, in which each family has its own house, and the use of farm land to do with as it pleases. The people of the village have joined together, however, to buy farm machinery and seeds for the use of all, and to sell the crops and dairy products. They jointly pay for doctors, nurses, teachers, and men to manage the village stores. And, of course, there are villages in which nothing is owned jointly. They are very much like villages in the United States.

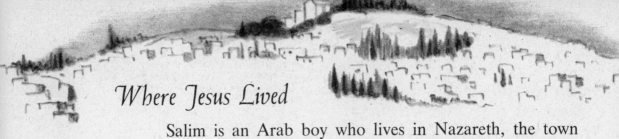

Where Jesus Lived

Salim is an Arab boy who lives in Nazareth, the town where Jesus lived as a boy. Nazareth, crowned with church towers, perches on a hill in Galilee, a district in northern Israel. In spring the Galilean hills are an Oriental carpet of yellow jonquils, purple hyacinths and blue lupins.

Salim's family lives in a very old house with a raised platform at one end for sleeping. The other end is occupied by the family goats and chickens. Salim's father is a carpenter, as Jesus was. His small dark shop faces a cobbled lane where there are stalls of vegetables and mounds of "pita," the flat unleavened bread loaf said to be the original matza. The lane twists and turns, hardly wide enough for people on foot to get by those astride donkeys so tiny the riders' feet almost touch the ground.

Salim's parents are Moslems. His father wears a flowing headdress and a long striped robe over baggy trousers. His mother is veiled in black from head to foot when she goes out, because according to Moslem custom, her face must not be seen in public. But Salim himself dresses like an American or an Israeli child, and his sister probably will never wear a face veil. For even Arab Nazareth is changing under the Israel government. The children no longer have sicknesses that come from ignorance and dirt. They go to public schools where lessons are in Arabic, and Hebrew is also taught.

Nazareth has its own local government with an Arab mayor, Arab policemen and judges. Unlike Salim's family, most

56

of Nazareth's Arabs are Christians. In addition there is a large Christian population of monks, nuns, and the Fathers who act as guardians of the shrines.

Susan and her parents climbed up the hill to the Church of the Annunciation in Nazareth. It is built over the grotto where Mary, mother of Jesus, lived before her marriage to Joseph. In the Church of St. Joseph nearby they could see through a grating in the floor the childhood home of Jesus, a bare cave with storage pits for oil and grain, and a shelf for the lamp, carved out of the rock. They also saw the old synagogue, built over the ruins of an even older one where Jesus studied and later preached almost 2000 years ago.

Susan and her parents drove on to Tiberias, a Roman town on the Sea of Galilee, which is not a salt sea but a large fresh-water lake. Israelis call it Lake Kinnereth, and it is the subject of many lovely songs. Nearby are the ruins of Capernaum, the site of the miracle of the loaves and fishes. Jesus won the first disciples from among the fishermen of Capernaum.

Men Can Make the Rain Fall

It rains unevenly in Israel—there is too much water in the winter, and not enough for the rest of the year. In some places it is so dry and dusty that the Israelis tell jokes about it, like this one: "Last week a drop of water fell on a man. They had to throw three buckets of dust on him to revive him."

Once these dry hills were covered with forests. Neglected, and chopped down for firewood, the trees disappeared. Once the stony fields were good pasture land. The Arabs' goats nibbled the grass almost down to bare rock.

Trees and grass hold water. Without them the winter rains cause floods, but when summer comes again, the water has

58

vanished, taking the rich topsoil with it, leaving only dry ditches and cracks in the earth, called "wadis."

One of the first things the Jewish pioneers did was to plant trees. Where they have grown big, the soil is better already. Jews all over the world remember birthdays, holidays, or the death of a loved one by giving money to "plant a tree in Israel." Many of these trees are planted by children on Arbor Day.

Along the roads leading south, you will see workmen tenderly watering young seedlings of the eucalyptus, a tree which has proved its sturdiness in other dry climates. Last year's saplings will be proudly pointed out. Someday these too will bring shade to the sun-baked fields and dusty roads.

OTHER FESTIVALS IN ISRAEL

The Arabs of Israel celebrate all their Moslem festivals. Their holy month is Ramadan, during which they fast each day from 3 A.M. till sunset. The beginning of the fast is marked by the firing of guns.

One of the most interesting and mysterious folk of Israel are the Druses, who speak Arabic but are not Arabs. They fought on the side of Israel in the War for Independence. They live in the mountains of Galilee and across the border in Syria, and have their own religion. Their main holiday is Nebi Shu'eib, the feast of Jethro, faher-in-law of Moses, whom they believe to be the ancestor of all Druses.

All the usual Christian festivals are celebrated by the Christians in Israel. A special one is the pilgrimage by the Franciscan Fathers of Nazareth to Kfar Kanna, now an Arab village, to celebrate Jesus' first miracle: the changing of water into wine at a wedding in Cana. At Christmas, there are services in Jerusalem, Nazareth, and Bethlehem. (Bethlehem is in the part of Israel held by Transjordan.)

60

Where the Tribes Wandered in the Wilderness

The Negev makes up one half the land of Israel. Once it was called "the bread-basket of Israel." But after the trees were destroyed and the goats allowed to roam at will, nothing grew there but scanty grass, barely enough to feed the flocks of the Arab tribes which wandered from place to place. The Bedouins still live in the Negev with their sheep and goats and camels, camping in black goatskin tents just as the ancient Israelites did. But nowadays, encouraged by the Israel Government, a Bedouin may have a settled house as headquarters. If one of his many wives is sick, he will take her to a modern hospital supported by charitable American women in Beersheba, the capital town of the Negev. Beersheba, which looks not unlike a frontier town in a Western movie, does have water. Its name means "Seven Wells."

The new pioneers are building dams across the wadis to catch and hold the water of the brief but violent floods of winter. In the north of Israel a man-made lake is rising. Rivers are being harnessed and their courses changed so that they do not pour out wastefully into the sea. A huge pipe line of concrete carries water to the southland. And already the upper Negev is a prairie again, rippling with golden grain.

But there is still the real desert, the Arabah. Here not even grass grows. The ground is ash-white, and the barren mountains are red, gray and yellow. Here there are huge rocks, carved by wind and weather to look like monsters and ancient castles.

61

Here you see distant columns of dust, whirling away by themselves, which explain the "pillar of cloud by day" with which God guided the people of Moses.

But there are rich minerals in this wilderness which modern science can put to use. There is a seven-mile long hole in the earth called "the Big Crater," from which the Israelis are digging material for pottery, tiles and bathtubs. The Dead Sea, which is very salty, lies in the lowest spot on earth. In spite of the fiery heat, workers there are taking out chemicals for plant fertilizer, cattle food, and washing detergents. At the very southern tip of Israel, copper is being mined for the first time since King Solomon's day.

Even in the real desert, plants will grow if water can be found to irrigate the rich soil. If you were to drive south from Beersheba, you would see crews of men prospecting for deep hidden springs as if they were gold mines. Americans, who have so much water, forget that it is the most precious fluid in the world.

Soldier of Israel

Deborah is a soldier. Because Israel is so small and surrounded by enemies, it must have a strong, wide-awake army. When they are eighteen, all boys and girls are called up for the army.

Deborah is on frontier service. This is actually farm work with a few days each month given to military exercises. She is stationed at a new settlement in the Negev where experiments are being made with plants that will stand desert heat and dryness. Only young people have the courage and strength to undertake this job, working in the blazing sun, sleeping in crude huts without comforts, far away from civilization and family.

The Israeli pioneers must constantly be on the watch for Arab marauders who slip across the border to attack workers in lonely outposts. Deborah knows how to handle a gun as well as a boy. The army insignia she wears on her uniform is an olive branch, the symbol of peace, crossed with a sword.

Deborah is very proud of what she is doing. She feels that she is helping to make Israel a nation strong enough to carry out its ideas of freedom, democracy, and justice for all.

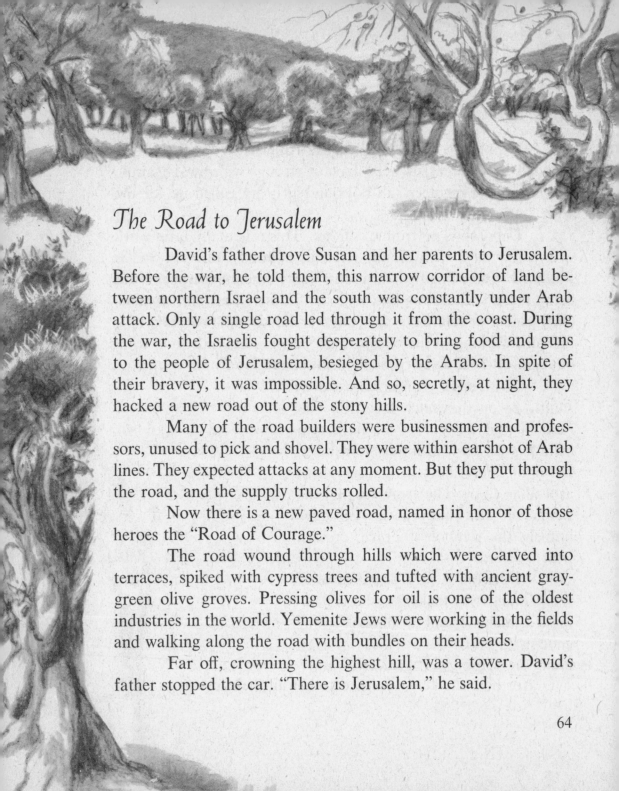

The Road to Jerusalem

David's father drove Susan and her parents to Jerusalem. Before the war, he told them, this narrow corridor of land between northern Israel and the south was constantly under Arab attack. Only a single road led through it from the coast. During the war, the Israelis fought desperately to bring food and guns to the people of Jerusalem, besieged by the Arabs. In spite of their bravery, it was impossible. And so, secretly, at night, they hacked a new road out of the stony hills.

Many of the road builders were businessmen and professors, unused to pick and shovel. They were within earshot of Arab lines. They expected attacks at any moment. But they put through the road, and the supply trucks rolled.

Now there is a new paved road, named in honor of those heroes the "Road of Courage."

The road wound through hills which were carved into terraces, spiked with cypress trees and tufted with ancient gray-green olive groves. Pressing olives for oil is one of the oldest industries in the world. Yemenite Jews were working in the fields and walking along the road with bundles on their heads.

Far off, crowning the highest hill, was a tower. David's father stopped the car. "There is Jerusalem," he said.

64

The City of King David

Jerusalem stands on hills guarded by other hills: the Mount of Olives, with church towers and dark cypresses pointing heavenward; Mount Scopus, with the gleaming modern buildings of the Hebrew University and the great Hadassah Hospital. Jerusalem itself has two parts.

The Old City is a honeycomb of stone, of houses built on top of older houses, of roof-tops and underground passages. Encircled by a medieval wall, it looks like an enchanted storybook city. And it *is* an enchanted city. Most of it has been pulled down, set on fire, strewn with salt so nothing green would grow again—and it has risen many times. It is one of the oldest cities in which people still live, four thousand years old at least. It was old when King David made it the capital city of his kingdom and built his fortress on Mount Zion.

And it is the Holy City of three religions. There King Solomon built the First Temple, with a great rock as foundation for the altar. Moslems believe that Mohammed, their prophet, went up to heaven on a winged horse from this same rock. Jesus preached and died in Old Jerusalem. One piece of wall, the only thing there is left of the Second Temple, is known as the Wailing Wall, for here the Jews returned to bewail their loss.

65

They dreamed always of Jerusalem, the sacred city. There was an ancient legend that Israel was the center of the world and Jerusalem the center of this center. About a hundred years ago, so many people had come back to live in Jerusalem that they spilled over into a settlement outside the walls. This was the start of the New City. So you will find in Jerusalem every kind of Jew from every part of the globe, and belonging to many different kinds of synagogues. You will see bearded Jews with frock coats and flat beaver hats, with a curl dangling over each ear. You will see European and American Jews in clothes no different from those you would see on the streets of New York. In the Oriental Quarter, the women wear flowing gowns and big dangling earrings. The men wear skirts over their pants, turbans or fur caps on their heads. Their market stalls are full of strange things to eat: spices and sweet pastes, dried figs and dates.

In New Jerusalem, there are also up-to-date hotels and apartment houses, schools and parks, government buildings, and a busy shopping center. There is a museum of ancient Jewish art and a modern art school. On Mount Scopus is a museum of every plant and flower mentioned in the Bible. There are theaters, concert halls, hospitals and banks. There is, in fact, almost everything you'd find in any big city, plus some things you'd find almost nowhere else in the world.

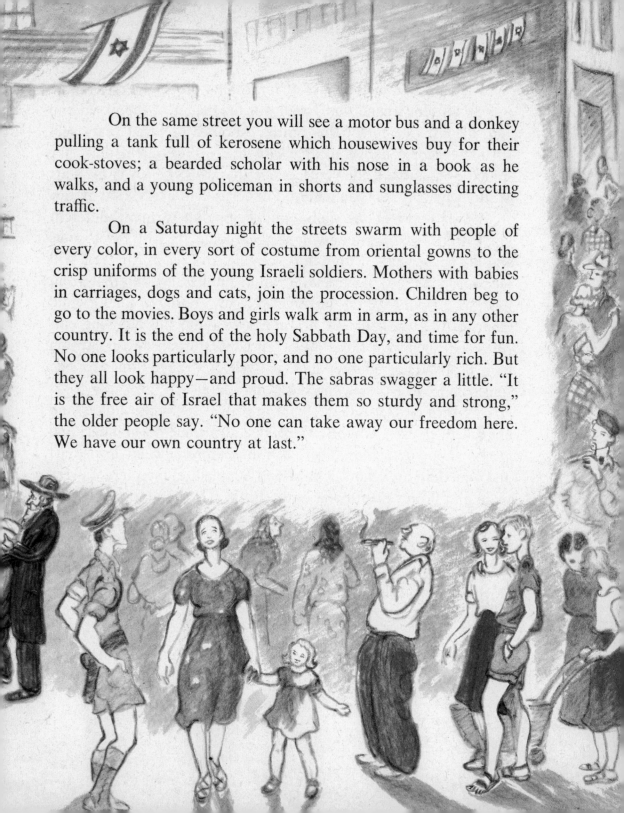

On the same street you will see a motor bus and a donkey pulling a tank full of kerosene which housewives buy for their cook-stoves; a bearded scholar with his nose in a book as he walks, and a young policeman in shorts and sunglasses directing traffic.

On a Saturday night the streets swarm with people of every color, in every sort of costume from oriental gowns to the crisp uniforms of the young Israeli soldiers. Mothers with babies in carriages, dogs and cats, join the procession. Children beg to go to the movies. Boys and girls walk arm in arm, as in any other country. It is the end of the holy Sabbath Day, and time for fun. No one looks particularly poor, and no one particularly rich. But they all look happy—and proud. The sabras swagger a little. "It is the free air of Israel that makes them so sturdy and strong," the older people say. "No one can take away our freedom here. We have our own country at last."

Susan stood with her father on the terrace of the famous King David Hotel, looking across the garden of bright flower beds to the battlements and towers of the Old City. "It makes me feel strange and sort of shivery," she said, "to be in a place so old —and so—so full of history. But I think I understand why the Jews wanted to come back, don't you?"

Softly, her father quoted from a Psalm written during the Jewish exile by the rivers of Babylon: " 'If I forget thee, O Jerusalem, let my right hand forget her cunning.' Yes, I understand. And we will wish for the new nation to be successful in what it promises to do for all who live here, and as a member of the family of nations."

INDEX